W9-BJN-258

DATE DUE

5563

582.16   Althea
A   Trees and leaves

Woodland Presbyterian School

NATURE CLUB

TREES
AND
LEAVES

ALTHEA

Illustrated by
DAVID MORE

Woodland Presbuterian School

Troll Associates

5563

Nature Club Notes

Look around you. How many things can you see that come from trees? You may be surprised.... Did you include this book, or the plastic on your pen?

Trees are important to people in all kinds of ways. You can grow your own tree very easily. All you need to do is plant the seeds from the fruit you eat, or seeds that have fallen from the trees in the fall. Sprinkle a layer of small stones in a container. Then fill it with fine earth or seed compost. Plant your seed and cover it with another layer of soil. Place a piece of plastic wrap or a plastic bag over the container, to keep the seed warm and moist. But remember to remove the plastic when the shoot breaks through the soil. It will need to be watered regularly if it is to grow.

To recognize the trees you see, and the birds and other animals that live on them, you will need some reference books. A pocket magnifying glass will help you identify tiny insects and other small creatures. It will also enable you to examine the scales on a leaf bud. A lot of life goes on in just one tree!

By pressing leaves and drawing pictures you can make your own book about trees. You may also want to keep a diary of one tree throughout the year, noting all the animals you see on it, and when it has flowers or fruits. Many people think that buds form in the spring, but Nature Club members will have used their magnifying glass and seen that they were there the previous year. This book tells how to make plaster casts of bark, but you can also make casts of fruit, seeds or leaves.

Trees can live for thousands of years. Your little shoot in a container could be the start of something big!

Library of Congress Cataloging-in-Publication Data

Althea.
    Trees & leaves / by Althea; illustrated by David More & Graham
Allen.
        p.   cm.—(The Nature club)
    Includes bibliographical references.
    Summary: Describes the characteristics of various trees and how
they provide food and shelter for animals.
    ISBN 0-8167-1967-5 (lib. bdg.)   ISBN 0-8167-1968-3 (pbk.)
    1. Trees—Juvenile literature.   2. Leaves—Juvenile literature.
[1. Trees.]   I. More, David, ill.   II. Allen, Graham, 1940-   ill.
III. Title.   IV. Title: Trees and leaves.   V. Series.
QK475.8.A473   1990
582.16—dc20   89-20308

Metric Equivalents

1 inch	=	25.4 mm
1 foot	=	30.5 cm
1 pint	=	.47 l
1 gallon	=	3.79 l

Published by Troll Associates

Text copyright © 1990 Althea Braithwaite

Illustrations copyright © Eagle Books Limited

All rights reserved. No part of this book may be reproduced or utilized in any form or by any means, electronic or mechanical, including photocopying, recording or by any storage and retrieval system, without permission in writing from the Publisher.

Designed by Cooper Wilson, London
Design consultant James Marks

Printed in the United States of America, bound in Mexico
10 9 8 7 6 5 4 3 2

Contents

What are Trees?

Trees are the giants of the plant world. They are so much bigger than other plants that they need a strong wooden stem, or *trunk*, to hold them up. They are the oldest, and largest, living things.

How good are you at identifying trees? Although the thousands of species may seem confusing, they are all divided into three main types – *broadleaved*, *conifers* and *palms*.

Beech

Oak

Broadleaved Trees

All the trees illustrated on this page have large, flat leaves. In the fall these will turn to shades of yellow, gold, orange, red or brown. Then they will fall from the tree. Trees that lose their leaves this way are called *deciduous*. Most broadleaved trees are deciduous. All broadleaved trees have flowers, from which they make seeds to grow new trees.

Conifers are another type of tree. They got their name because they make their seeds in cones, instead of producing them from flowers. Most conifers are evergreens.

Apple   Sycamore   Hawthorn

Are all Conifers Evergreens?

These trees are conifers. The larch is, too, but it sheds its needle-like leaves in the fall. So the answer to the above question is no.

Evergreens do shed old leaves, but not just in the fall, as deciduous trees do. Evergreens produce new leaves before the old ones fall.

The tough leaves of evergreens can stand extremes of temperature. High in the mountains you are likely to find only conifers. If you examine their shape you will see that they are better able to cope with snow than deciduous trees are.

The Norway Spruce is often used as a Christmas tree.

Norway Spruce   Douglas Fir   Giant Sequoia

The Giant Sequoia has tiny leaves along its stem.

Grand Fir. When crushed the leaves smell of tangerines.

Live Oak

Cork Oak

Holly

Monkey Puzzle

Yew

7

Trees Grow from Seeds

"From little acorns do mighty oaks grow" is a common saying. Oak trees live for up to 1,000 years. Yet, like all trees, they start from a tiny seed.

Seeds need enough sunlight and water from the soil to grow. Seeds grow better away from the shadow of their parent, so nature finds ways to scatter them.

Maples produce seeds with wings to be blown by the wind. A squirrel buries nuts for the winter, when food is scarce. If he forgets one, he may have planted a tree. Birds eat berries, cherries, and other fruit. Either they spit the seed out, or it will pass through them, undigested, and be scattered in their droppings. Other seeds are carried on the water.

If you watch an acorn grow, you will see that it produces two shoots. Whichever way you plant the acorn, one shoot grows down to form a root and the other grows up to become a trunk.

Horse Chestnut

Oak

Beech

Oak

Beech

Hawthorn

Silver Birch

Most trees produce thousands of seeds each year, but only one seed needs to survive and grow for the tree to replace itself. Can you guess how the seeds on this page are spread?

Hazel

Alder

Maple

Maple

Apple

Hawthorn

Seeds in Cones

Cedar cones fall apart while still on the tree.

Conifer trees have male and female cones instead of flowers. You may have seen large quantities of fine yellow powder at the foot of a pine tree. This is pollen from the male cones. It is carried to the female cones by the wind.

Female cones are larger than male cones. Once pollinated, they begin to harden and close up. They can remain closed for several years while the seeds ripen inside. On a warm day, when the cone is ready, it will open to allow its single-winged seeds to be carried away by the wind. One Californian bristlecone pine is nearly 5,000 years old. The tallest tree, a coast redwood, is 362 feet (110 m) high. Both were once seeds in cones.

Some cones, like that of the lodgepole pine, only release their seeds after a fire. This is nature's way of re-creating a forest after it has been burned.

You can collect cones to help you identify trees, or paint them as Christmas decorations.

Bishop Pine. The cone remains on the tree for up to 25 years. It only releases its seeds to grow new trees after the heat of a forest fire.

Douglas Fir

Stone Pine seed

Scotch Pine

10

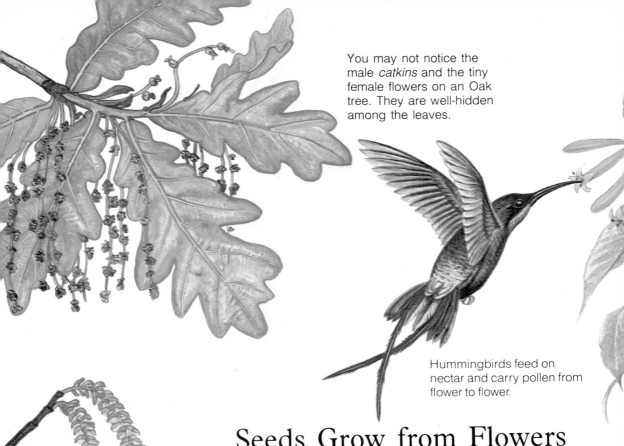

You may not notice the male *catkins* and the tiny female flowers on an Oak tree. They are well-hidden among the leaves.

Hummingbirds feed on nectar and carry pollen from flower to flower.

The *catkins* hanging from the Hazel tree are its male flowers. The female flower is on the same twig. It has a sticky red part to catch pollen from the catkin if they brush against one another in the wind.

Seeds Grow from Flowers

All broadleaved trees are flowering plants. Larger tree blossoms, like the magnolia, may have both male and female parts in the same flower. But some trees with smaller blossoms have male flowers on one tree and female flowers on another. *Pollen*, a fine powder produced by the male part, must join with the female part of a blossom for a seed to be created. This is called *pollination*.

Insects feeding on *nectar* (the honey produced by plants) in the blossom may carry the sticky pollen from the male to the female flower. Trees with smaller flowers often rely on the wind to perform this task for them.

Buds-Next Season's Leaves

After a tree's leaves have dropped you will need new tricks to recognize it. Looking at its buds is one way to identify a deciduous tree. Conifer buds are so small they aren't much help. Buds contain all of next season's twigs, leaves, or flowers, neatly folded into packages.

Buds are protected from drying out by scales, hairs, and sticky coats. Can you spot the differences among the twigs shown on this page?

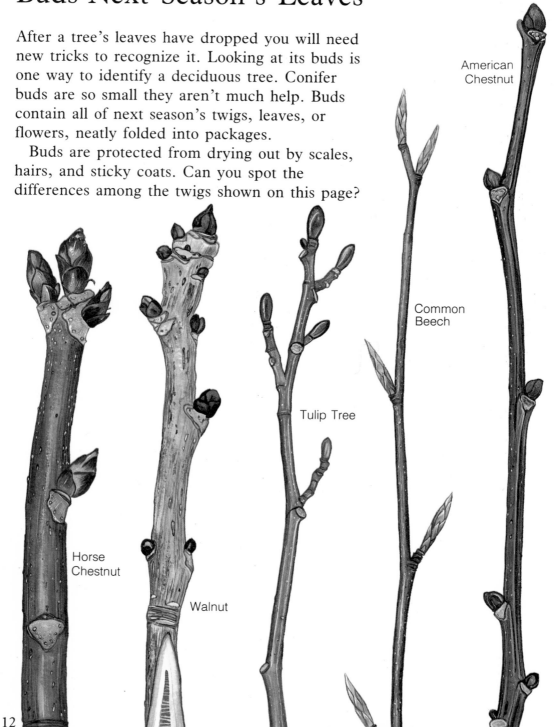

American Chestnut

Common Beech

Tulip Tree

Horse Chestnut

Walnut

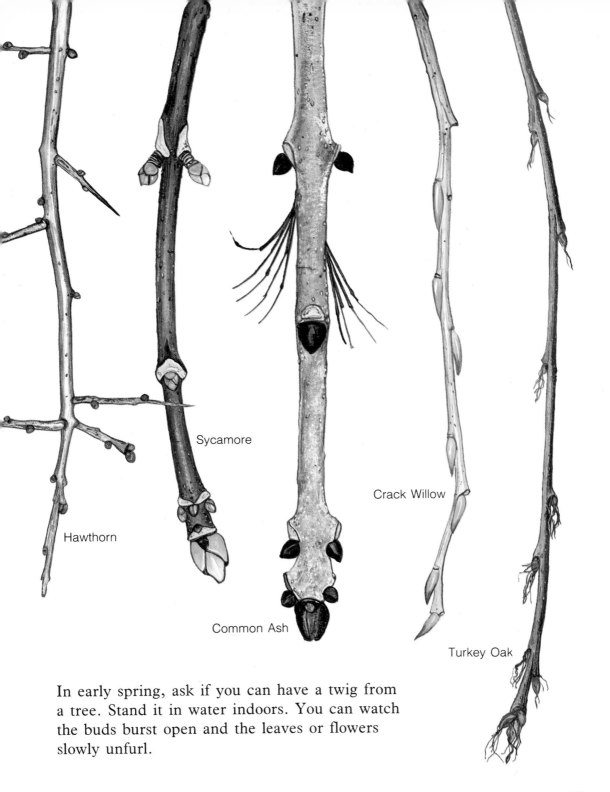

Sycamore

Crack Willow

Hawthorn

Common Ash

Turkey Oak

In early spring, ask if you can have a twig from
a tree. Stand it in water indoors. You can watch
the buds burst open and the leaves or flowers
slowly unfurl.

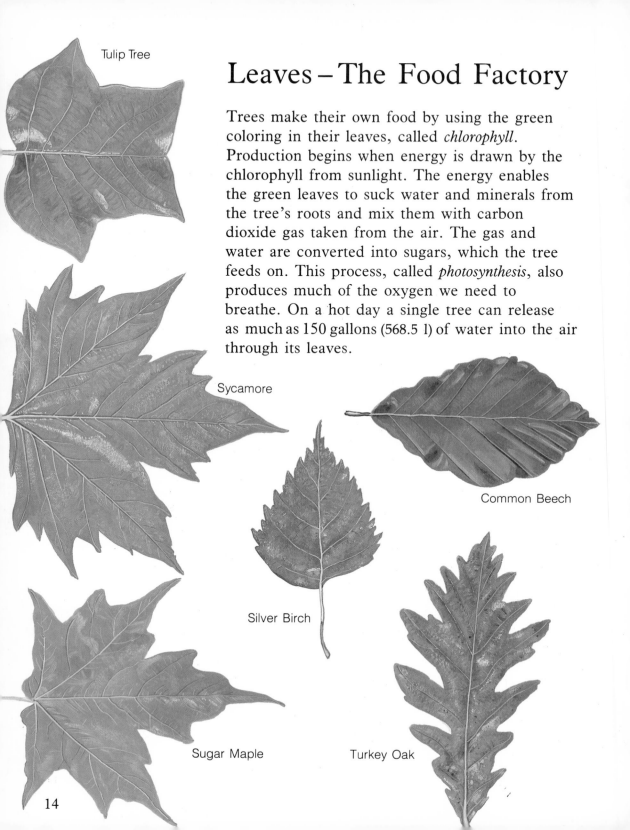

Tulip Tree

Leaves – The Food Factory

Trees make their own food by using the green coloring in their leaves, called *chlorophyll*. Production begins when energy is drawn by the chlorophyll from sunlight. The energy enables the green leaves to suck water and minerals from the tree's roots and mix them with carbon dioxide gas taken from the air. The gas and water are converted into sugars, which the tree feeds on. This process, called *photosynthesis*, also produces much of the oxygen we need to breathe. On a hot day a single tree can release as much as 150 gallons (568.5 l) of water into the air through its leaves.

Sycamore

Common Beech

Silver Birch

Sugar Maple

Turkey Oak

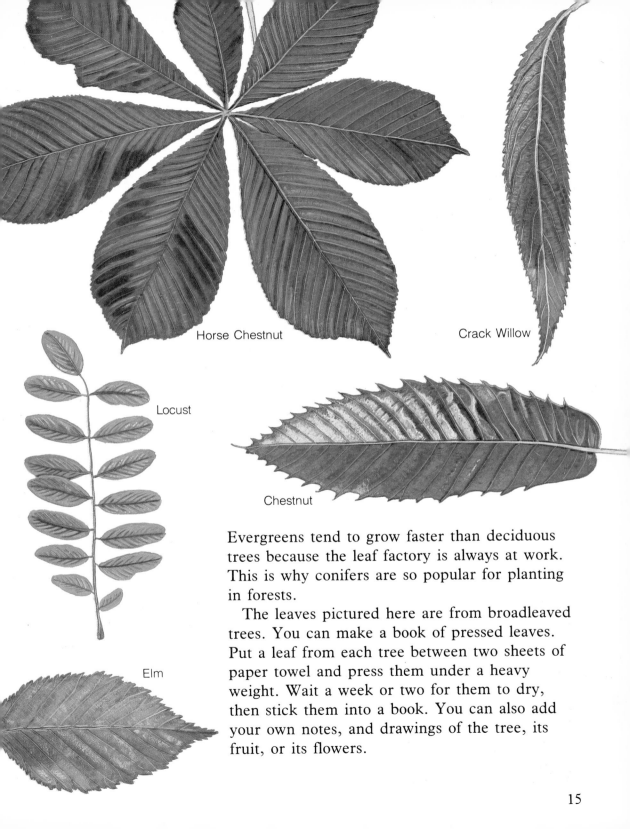

Horse Chestnut

Crack Willow

Locust

Chestnut

Elm

Evergreens tend to grow faster than deciduous trees because the leaf factory is always at work. This is why conifers are so popular for planting in forests.

The leaves pictured here are from broadleaved trees. You can make a book of pressed leaves. Put a leaf from each tree between two sheets of paper towel and press them under a heavy weight. Wait a week or two for them to dry, then stick them into a book. You can also add your own notes, and drawings of the tree, its fruit, or its flowers.

Fall Colors

In the fall the deciduous tree prepares for winter, and begins to "close up shop." It cannot afford to give off water through its leaves if it is unable to replace it with water from the ground, which may be frozen. As photosynthesis stops, the tree withdraws the supply of water and minerals, known as *sap*, from the leaves and seals off the passages to the leaves. As the green chlorophyll fades, the fall colors, which were always in the leaves, start to show.

Sugar Maple

Silver Birch

Common Beech

Tulip Tree

Silver Birch

Sycamore

Shapes of Trees

Each type of tree has a distinctive shape that will help you to recognize it. But the shape can vary, depending on where the tree is growing.

Trees growing close together in the woods are often too squashed to take on their natural shape. If they are crowded, they must grow tall and spindly if they are to reach the light.

Trees that grow in cold or windy conditions, or on coasts or mountains, may be shorter and have branches pointing in the same direction as the winds blow.

Other trees may have had their shape changed by animals eating their lower leaves or destroying their bottom branches. People cut back trees to keep them from growing too tall. Fruit trees may also be trimmed, or pruned, to make fruit-picking easier.

Crack Willow which has been cut.

Tree growing tall to reach the light.

Windswept tree   Meadow tree eaten by cattle

The Trunk of the Tree

The trunk is the strong, woody stem. The hard center, or *heartwood*, of the trunk is what holds the tree upright. Each spring new activity under the bark enables the tree to continue to grow. The layer inside the bark, called the *cambium*, grows a new ring of woody tubes called *sapwood*. These tubes carry water and minerals up the trunk from the roots. The fibrous layer inside the bark carries water mixed with food down from the leaves to the roots. This water and food mixture is called *sap*.

By late summer the cambium growth slows down and the woody tubes are smaller and darker. If you find a tree stump, you can count the rings to find the age of the tree. Each light and dark ring represents one year of growth. Most trees expand by about 1 inch (2.54 cm) each year.

Enlarged picture of sapwood to show the hollow tubes which carry the sap up the tree.

A tree need not be cut down to find its age. A cylinder of wood is removed by boring a hole to the trunk's center, so the rings can be counted.

1 Bark   2 Fibrous layer

3 Cambium   4 Sapwood

5 Heartwood

The Bark

Bark is the outer wood of the trunk and branches. It protects the tree from losing too much water. The tree breathes through tiny holes in the bark. Some trees shed a thin layer of bark each year to get rid of dirt and dust. Because bark is a dead layer it cannot grow; so as the tree gets older and its trunk thickens, the bark cracks or falls off. The bark of each kind of tree has its own pattern of cracks and ridges. This is another clue to recognizing different types of trees.

Rubbings can be made of bark patterns. Tape a sheet of paper to the bark and rub all over the paper evenly with a wax crayon. The pattern of the bark will come up on the paper. Very rough bark will tear the paper, so you can make a plaster cast of the pattern instead. Press a flattened piece of modeling clay firmly into the bark. Then peel off the clay very carefully. Take the mold home and build up its sides with more clay. Then pour some quick-drying plaster of Paris into the mold. When it is dry and hard, carefully peel off the clay. Finally, you can paint and varnish the cast.

Turkey Oak

Chestnut

Woodland Presbyterian School

White Ash

Silver Birch

Apple

Coast Redwood

Roots as Anchors

If trees had no roots they would fall over! Roots form the tree's anchor. The main root is called the *taproot*. It can grow deep into the soil. Closer to the surface, trees spread out an enormous web of roots. Some trees have more growth underground than above.

The art of growing miniature trees, called *bonsai*, has been perfected by the Japanese. To keep the trees small, they trim their roots. It takes as long to grow a bonsai as it does a normal-size tree.

Bonsai

Beech

Millions of tiny hairs grow near the tips of a tree's roots to soak up water and minerals from the soil. They deliver this water through the trunk to the leaves.

Although trees need large amounts of water, their roots also need air. Most trees are unable to grow where the earth is always waterlogged. Some trees solve this problem by growing roots above the ground, like stilts.

There are trees whose roots seem to have a life of their own. If the tree is felled, the roots send up new trunks and leaves. These new growths, called *suckers*, will grow into full-size trees.

If you would like to see a root system grow, fill a narrow-necked bottle with water. Balance an acorn on the top of the bottle. If necessary, secure it with modeling clay. The acorn will grow a taproot first. Since it cannot live on just water forever, plant it in a container before the root system grows too big.

Mangrove

The woodpecker pecks away to make a hole big enough for its family.

Pine martens and weasels climb trees in search of birds' eggs or newly hatched chicks.

Birds and Other Animals

As well as feeding on the fruits and nuts growing on trees, many animals make their homes there. Birds nest among the branches. It is a good place to hide.

Squirrels build their nests high up in trees.

Owls and bats make their homes in trees too.

Brown creepers run around and up the trunk, using their slender beak to feed on small insects that live in the cracks of the bark.

Howler and squirrel monkeys feed on fruit.

A sloth hangs by its feet from the branches as it feeds.

Hornbills nest in holes in tropical trees. To keep their eggs safe, the male helps the female seal herself into the nest by closing up the entrance with clay and droppings. They leave a narrow slit, so he can pass food to her while she hatches the eggs.

When you examine the leaves on a tree you may find some of them have been eaten. Perhaps you will find some caterpillars munching their way through the leaves. Trees keep spare buds in reserve to replace leaves which have been eaten.

You might like to keep the caterpillars in a jar to watch them grow and change into pupae. The pupa protects the caterpillar while it develops wings and changes into an adult insect. Provide a layer of soil at the bottom of their new home, since some caterpillars hide under the soil to pupate. Each day they will need fresh leaves from the tree on which you found them.

Oak Apple gall

Oak Apple gall. This gall is divided into chambers and there may be up to 30 larvae living in it.

The purple hairstreak caterpillar and butterfly live on the Oak tree.

Gall wasp

Spangle galls grow on the underside of the leaf in the fall. When the wasps emerge in the spring they lay eggs on the catkin of the oak tree. These produce currant galls, from which wasps emerge in the summer.

Cherry galls can be found on the lower side of an oak leaf in the fall.

As many as 500 different types of small animals may live on just one oak tree!

You may find growths called *galls* on a tree's leaves, or attached to the twigs. These are home to even more tiny animals. The growth is caused by an insect boring into the leaves or twigs to lay her eggs. When the larva, or grub, hatches and begins to grow, the tree forms a gall around it. Both the larvae and their home may end up as food for other animals.

To see a gall wasp, collect some galls in spring or summer and put them in a jar with a screen over the top. A gall with a hole in it is no good, because the wasp has already flown away.

Pineapple galls are common on spruce trees. They are caused by aphids and each may have up to a hundred aphids living in its separate cavities.

Fruit and Nuts

The seeds that grow from flowers are sometimes protected by fruit, many of which are good to eat.

After enjoying the fruit, try planting the seeds in flowerpots to grow your own trees. Soak the larger seeds in hot water overnight first. Cover the pot with plastic wrap or a plastic bag to keep the soil moist and warm until the plants start to grow.

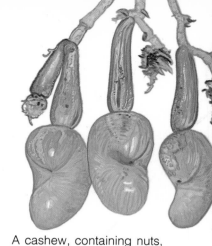

A cashew, containing nuts, hangs down from a fleshy fruit stalk.

You will find lots of ripe brown seeds inside these apples and pears.

As well as being good to eat, walnuts, pecans and hazelnuts are all single seeds.

Plums, peaches, apricots and cherries each contain one large seed.

Litchis, mangoes and avocado pears contain a single seed.

The hard woody case of the Brazil nut encloses 12 to 24 nuts.

Most oranges, lemons and other citrus fruits have seeds in the middle.

Date

Clusters of dates hang
down among the leaves
of the Date palm.

Palm Trees

Palms make up a third group of trees. They
grow in warm climates, from a long stem or a
shorter, thicker stalk. Instead of branches, most
have a single bud at the top of the stem from
which a crown or fan of feather-shaped leaves
unfolds. Palm leaves can grow up to 50 feet (15 m).

The best known palms are dates and coconuts.
Coconut trees grow mostly in the tropics,
sometimes from nuts that have drifted across
oceans. Each tree provides 50-100 nuts a year.
Date palms are vital to desert dwellers,
providing food for them and their
animals. Their trunks are used
for building, and their leaves
for food and baskets.

Even when there is no
water, coconut milk inside
the nut can help the tree
start to grow. It is also good
to drink.

Products from Trees

Where would we be without wood? Almost everything our ancestors made was wooden. Wood fires warmed them and trees provided much of their food. Many products are now plastic, which is made from petroleum. Petroleum consists of the remains of many living things, buried deep underground.

Conifers, which take about 40 years to grow, are called *softwood trees*. Softwood is mainly used in building and for making paper. Broadleaved trees are called *hardwood trees*. Mahogany, ebony, and oak are all hardwoods that are becoming scarce. Because hardwoods take so long to grow, we must be careful how we use them. We must also plant new trees for future generations.

Tropical rain forests have a cooling effect on the atmosphere all around the world, but they are being destroyed at an alarming rate. Without trees, lands flood easily. Trees are vital to the world – to animals and plants, as well as ourselves, so we need to make sure that forests survive.

Tea is made from the leaves of a tree. To make it easier for the pickers, the trees are pruned to keep them small. The tips of the leaves produce the best tea.

Trees can be cut in different ways to show off the grain of the wood.

Mahogany

Sycamore

Yew

Walnut

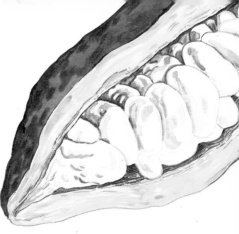

The fruit and flowers of the Cacao tree grow on the trunk of the tree. The pods contain 40 to 60 cocoa beans. They are used for making chocolate.

A nutmeg is covered with a layer of red mace, which turns brown during processing. Both nutmeg and mace are used in cooking.

Cork, which is used for cork tiles, is a layer of bark from the Cork Oak.

Cinnamon sticks are the bark of young shoots of the cinnamon tree. The bark curls up as it dries.

Coffee berries each contain two coffee beans.

Syrup is collected from the Sugar Maple. The bark is tapped and the sugary sap drips into a small bucket. It takes about 40 pints (19 l) of sap to make one pint of maple syrup.

Glossary

bark   the covering on the outside of the tree that protects it from heat or cold and from animals.

bonsai   a tree grown in a container, which is kept artificially small by trimming both its roots and branches.

broadleaved tree   a tree that has wide flat leaves. Broadleaved trees all produce flowers in order to make seeds. Most broadleaved trees are deciduous.

cambium   the layer just under the bark which starts growing a ring of new food-carrying tubes each year. Cambium is also found at the growing tips of shoots and roots.

catkin   a cluster of small male or female flowers that are wind-pollinated.

chlorophyll   the green coloring in leaves and other green parts of a plant.

conifer   a tree that bears cones. Most conifer trees have leaves like needles or small scales, and many are also evergreen.

deciduous   a tree or shrub that loses its leaves at the end of the growing season, leaving it leafless during the winter.

evergreen   a tree that is green throughout the year, even during the winter and dry seasons. It loses a few leaves at a time, but new ones grow before the old leaves are shed.

gall   a growth caused by an insect boring into a plant to lay her eggs.

hardwood   the wood from broadleaved trees. Hardwood trees take many hundreds of years to grow.

heartwood   the dead wood at the center of the tree which no longer carries sap. It becomes very hard and keeps the tree strong and upright.

nectar   a sugary liquid, like honey, which is produced by flowering plants.

palm   a tree growing up on a stout stem with a single bud which unfolds into a crown of very long fan- or feather-shaped leaves.

photosynthesis   the process by which chlorophyll in leaves uses light to convert carbon dioxide into foods.

pollen   fine yellow grain from male flowers that must join with the female part of a blossom to make a seed.

pollination   the joining of the male pollen and the female egg in a flower to create a seed.

sap   liquid food and water being carried around a tree.

sapwood   rings of living woody tubes through which water from the soil flows up to the leaves.

softwood   the term used for wood from conifers. Most conifers grow too quickly to form large hard trunks.

suckers   a shoot growing directly from the root or base of the stem.

taproot   the main downward-growing root of a tree.

trunk   the woody stem of a tree.

Index